SPREAD the Word

by Ciaran Murtagh

OXFORD
UNIVERSITY PRESS
AUSTRALIA & NEW ZEALAND

OXFORD
UNIVERSITY PRESS

Oxford University Press is a department of the University of Oxford.
It furthers the University's objective of excellence in research,
scholarship, and education by publishing worldwide. Oxford is a
registered trademark of Oxford University Press in the UK and in
certain other countries.

Published in Australia by
Oxford University Press
Level 8, 737 Bourke Street, Docklands, Victoria 3008, Australia

First published 2014
This edition 2019
Reprinted 2021 (twice)

ISBN 9780190317997

Series Editor: Nikki Gamble
Illustrations by Glen McBeth
Printed in China by Leo Paper Products Ltd

*Links to third party websites are provided by Oxford in good faith and
for information only. Oxford disclaims any responsibility for the materials
contained in any third party website referenced in this work.*

Acknowledgements

Cover artwork by Glen McBeth

The publishers would like to thank the following for the permission
to reproduce photographs:

p5t: Fotolibra; p5l: alamy/Pictorial press Ltd; **p5b:** Getty Images/
Hank Morgan/Science Faction; **p6t:** Fotolibra; **p6m:** mary Evans
picture Library; **p9:** Alamy/NTPL/Mark Fiennes; **p11:** Quang Ho/
Shutterstock; **p12l:** Alamy/Pictorial press Ltd; **p12r:** Getty Images;
p13: Getty Images/Time Life Pictures; **p15:** Alamy/Picture Library;
p16l: Science Museum/Science and Society Picture Library;
p16r: Science Museum/Science and Society Picture Library;
p16b: Mary Evans picture Library; **p17tl:** Basement Stock/Alamy;
p17bl: Science Museum/Science and Society Picture Library;
p17br: Alamy/Pumpkin Pie; **p17tr:** Shutterstock/Christopher Dodge;
p18: Getty Images/Hank Morgan/Science Faction; **Background
images:** Thaiview/Shutterstock; Semisatch/Shutterstock; saicle/
Shutterstock; arigato/Shutterstock; skyboysv/Shutterstock.

We have made every effort to trace and contact all copyright holders
before publication. If notified, the publisher will rectify any errors
or omissions at the earliest opportunity.

Contents

eetings!

Howdy!

Hi!

Introduction

People **communicate** all the time. Especially me! I'm always trying to spread the word. Sometimes I tap words into an email or a text. Sometimes I talk to people face to face. Sometimes I speak to people using a phone. And sometimes I spread the word through a book – like this!

How many ways am I spreading the word here?

Which are the best for long distances?

Which are the friendliest?

Which are the fastest?

But I wouldn't be able to do half of these things if it hadn't been for:

William Caxton,

Alexander Graham Bell

and **Tim Berners-Lee**.

They found ways to help spread the word all around the world.

William Caxton

What: **The printing press**

When: **The 1400s**

Nobody knows exactly when William Caxton was born.

It could have been 1419. Or maybe 1420 … ?

It was about 1421. ★

He grew up in Kent, England, then went to London to train to be a **merchant**.

Caxton sold British wool and bought **goods** from other European countries. On his travels, Caxton saw a printing press printing a book.

Without a printing press, if you wanted a book, you had to pay someone to write it out for you. This took a long time and cost lots of money.

With the printing press, it got quicker and cheaper to make books.

I'd like a book, please.

Come back in a year!

Caxton realised what an important invention the printing press was and he learned how to use it. ★

An early printing press

1. The printer put letters on a board to spell out words.

Messy business!

2. He covered the letters in ink and pulled down on a handle.

Beard at risk!

3. The inky letters were pressed onto a piece of paper and a page in a book was made.

Ta-da!

In 1476, Caxton set up a printing press in London. One of the first books printed in England was *The Canterbury Tales* by Geoffrey Chaucer. It was so popular that another version was printed with pictures!

Thanks to Caxton's printing press, more people could afford to buy books – although they were still quite expensive. And there wasn't much choice at first!

Caxton printed about 100 different books. Now millions of books are printed all around the world every year. Printing presses are faster and books are cheaper.

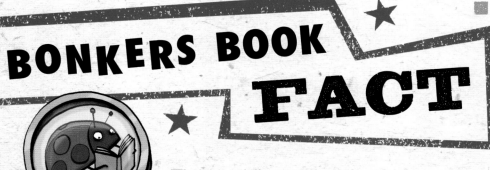

BONKERS BOOK FACT

The world's smallest book is *Shiki no Kusabana*. It's a Japanese book of flowers with pages less than 1 mm big!

In fact, without printing presses, you wouldn't be holding this book in your hand right now!

Alexander Graham Bell

What: **The telephone**

When: **The late 1800s**

Alexander Graham Bell was born in Edinburgh, Scotland, in 1847. He began inventing when he was just a boy.

12-year-old Bell and his first invention – a de-husking machine.

Bell

A school for the deaf in Boston, United States of America (USA)

When Bell grew up, he gave lessons to deaf people to help them communicate better. He worked in Canada and the USA. It was in the USA that Bell invented the telephone.

Bell wanted to find a way to talk to people who were a long way away. He invented something that would allow his voice to travel great distances.

On 10th March 1876, Bell used a telephone wire to send a message to his assistant in the next room. He said, "Mr Watson, come here. I want to see you!"

You could have just come and talked to me!

It was the first phone call! However, there was still a lot of work to do before Bell had made an actual telephone.

Bell's first telephone

Telephones helped people to communicate with each other more quickly and easily than ever before.

Over the years, telephones got better and better, and worked over longer and longer distances.

1890

1929

1954

Bell's other great inventions:

One of the first **metal detectors**

A record-breaking **hydrofoil** boat

A tool to find icebergs

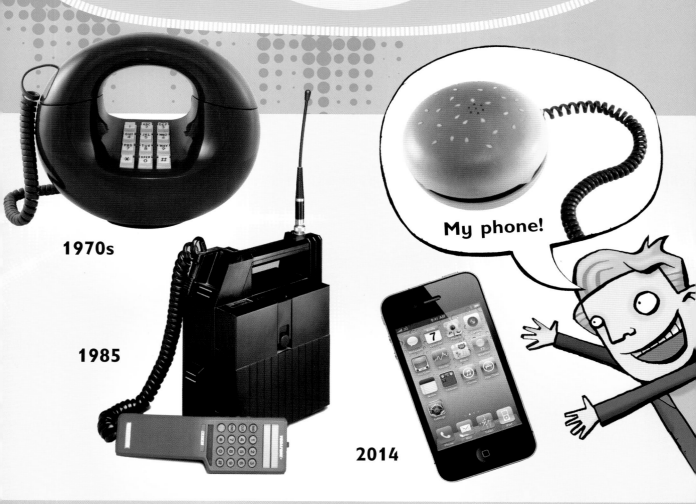

1970s

1985

2014

My phone!

Tim Berners-Lee

What: **The World Wide Web**

When: **The early 1990s**

Tim Berners-Lee was born in London, UK, in 1955. When he was a child, he was a keen **trainspotter**. He learned about **electronics** by playing with his model train set.

Berners-Lee went to study at Oxford University.

He became very interested in computers. He even built a computer out of an old television and a **processor**.

Hey! We were watching that!

Berners-Lee wanted to find a way of using computers to communicate with people all over the world quickly and for free. This is how he came up with the World Wide Web.

The World Wide Web is a way for people to use the **Internet** to communicate with each other. Lots of information is joined together in a "web" and is shared on their computers.

To thank Berners-Lee for his ideas and hard work, Queen Elizabeth II made him a **knight** in 2004.

Today, Berners-Lee works with people from around the world to improve the World Wide Web.

Glossary

communicate: to share information

electronics: the science of electricity

goods: items that can be bought or sold

husk: the shell around a grain of wheat

hydrofoil: a boat with wings that lift the boat out of the water

Internet: network of computers

knight: someone who is given a special honour by a king or queen

merchant: a person who sells goods to another person

metal detectors: machines that help people to find metal objects

processor: a machine that handles information

trainspotter: a person who spots trains for a hobby

Index